It's a Guy Thing: Let's Talk About Sex

Workbook

It's a Guy Thing: Let's Talk About Sex Workbook
Published by Guy Thing Press
P.O. Box 827
Roanoke, TX 76262

This book or parts thereof may not be reproduced in any form, stored in a retrieval system, or transmitted in any form by any means - electronic, mechanical, photocopy, recording, or otherwise - without prior written permission of the publisher, except as provided by United States of America copyright law.

Guy Thing Press books may be purchased in bulk for educational, business, fund-raising, or sales promotional use. For more information, please contact Guy Thing Press.

Please visit us at www.guythingpress.com

Copyright © 2008 by Guy Thing Press
All Rights Reserved

Printed in the United States of America

ISBN-13: 978-0-9818337-8-1
ISBN-10: 0-9818337-8-0

Part One - Let's Talk About Sex

Let's Talk About Sex...1

Sex and the Single Guy 7

Different from the Start..11

The Wonder of Sex..15

For the Clueless Bride 21

For the Clueless Groom 25

The Anatomy of Arousal 29

Scheduling Intimacy 33

The Bridge Between Touch and Sex 37

Setting the Scene 41

Sexual Stewardship 45

Is There Sex After Kids? 49

What's the Big Deal with Pornography?...............53

Toxic Sex 59

Infidelity - It's More Than Just Sex 63

Part Two - The Unhappy Gay Agenda

Once Gay Always Gay? 67

Gays in School: The Homosexual Agenda in Education 71

The Homosexual Agenda.................................. 75

The Homosexual Manifesto................................ 79

Part Three - Fatherhood Aborted

Fatherhood Aborted 83

When Daddy's Dream Died, Daddy Died Too 87

Help for Dads 91

Chapter One
Let's Talk About Sex

Let's Talk About Sex

1. What are the three common things that cause trouble in relationships?

_____

2. Love is about satisfying _____ at the expense of _____, because love desires to _____. Lust is satisfying _____ at the expense of _____, because lust desires to _____.

3. Summarize the three guidelines for sex.

_____

_____

_____

4. If masturbation is used as a way to _____ sex to your spouse, that would be destructive and go against the principles Paul describes in 1 Corinthians 7. If masturbation were accompanied by fantasies of _____ _____, then it would most certainly fit into the definition of lust found in Matthew 5.

5. What does the Bible say about sex between single people?

_____

_____

_____

6. There is _____ clear, biblical statement forbidding oral sex.

7. The Levitical laws, which deal with the most explicit sexual directives, do not mention anything about _____ _____.

Chapter One
Let's Talk About Sex

8. Sexual intimacy must always be based upon _____ and mutual _____.

9. Should we ever deny sex to our wife?

_____

10. What is the most intimate form of communication between a husband and wife?

_____

11. Sex toys can _____ be a substitute for human contact.

12. The so-called sex education video is just another term for _____.

13. Why is cyber-sex and phone sex adultery if not used within a marriage relationship?

_____

_____

_____

1 Corinthians 7:3–5:

The husband should fulfill his marital duty to his wife, and likewise the wife to her husband. The wife's body does not belong to her alone but also to her husband. In the same way, the husband's body does not belong to him alone but also to his wife. Do not deprive each other except by mutual consent and for a time, so that you may devote yourselves to prayer. Then come together again so that Satan will not tempt you because of your lack of self-control.

14. In what ways can we fulfill our marital duty to our wife?

_____

_____

_____

15. Define modesty.

_____
_____
_____

16. How can sex during menstruation be beneficial?

_____
_____
_____

17. What are some risks to having sex during menstruation?

_____
_____
_____

Chapter One
Let's Talk About Sex

Let's Talk About Sex

Chapter Two
Sex and the Single Guy

Let's Talk About Sex

1. We live in a _____ where sexual innuendo and lasciviousness are commonly used to _____ anything from breath mints to family detergent. _____ and purity are "simple concepts" that are openly scoffed at, blatantly _____, publicly _____, and held in derision.

2. What is the source of sex and how was it created to be?

_____

_____

_____

3. In what context should we judge sex?

_____

_____

_____

4. In marriage, the bed is _____.

5. Sex outside the marriage relationship is called _____ while single, and _____ when a marriage partner cheats on a spouse.

6. List the six guidelines to remember when with a female companion.

_____

_____

_____

_____

Chapter Two
Sex and the Single Guy

_____

_____

7. Can lust be satisfied?

_____

8. Why shouldn't someone locked in a loveless marriage commit adultery?

_____

_____

Chapter Three
Different from the Start

Let's Talk About Sex

1. The differences between the sexes were meant to bring _____ and _____ to human lives, not distraction and disturbance.

2. As men, we need to understand that God made men and women _____.

3. God did not create Eve from the dust of the earth as He did Adam. God took Eve out of _____.

4. In God are all the characteristics that make up the components of _____.

5. Being alone may be good for a season, but being _____ never is.

6. What happens when husband and wife become one flesh?

_____

_____

_____

7. A man who lives a _____ life does not bring glory to God and does not allow his wife to glory in him.

8. A woman's _____ is her greatest appeal to a man—and the greatest challenge he may ever face.

9. Adam was given the opportunity and the responsibility to oversee the process of _____ the earth.

10 Where does a man gain satisfaction and identification?

_____

_____

_____

Chapter Three
Different from the Start

11. The creative process for Adam was that he would plant his _____ in the woman Eve and the earth would be both _____ and _____ through this recreative act.

12. Woman was created to be _____ and to be _____ as the glory of God's creation, and as an object of love and affection for a man.

13. A woman needs more from her husband than just a _____ over her head and a _____ in the bed.

14. A young man needs to know how to be a _____ to a girl before he can ever qualify as a _____ to a woman.

15. Marriage does have its erotic and exotic moments, but those moments are not the basis or _____ upon which you can build a _____ of friendship.

Let's Talk About Sex

Chapter Four
The Wonder of Sex

Let's Talk About Sex

1. A photocopy of a photocopy of a photocopy ends up being nothing more than a _____ _____.

2. What is the issue with the degradation of sex?

_____

_____

_____

3. Satan cannot _____; he can only _____.

4. He will try to _____, _____, or _____ anything God creates.

5. Sex is the most potent act of _____ _____ between two people.

6. More than just a _____ act, it's a _____ of their spirits—the external expression of an internal _____.

7. What does covenant mean in the Hebrew language and what was its significance?

_____

_____

_____

8. For how long would a blood covenant be legally binding?

_____

Chapter Four
The Wonder of Sex

9. Describe the steps in the ceremony of covenant.

   1. Standing in the midst of the sacrifice

   _____

   _____

   _____

   2. Exchanging coats

   _____

   _____

   _____

   3. Exchange of weapons

   _____

   _____

   _____

   4. The walk of blood

   _____

   _____

   _____

5. The cut of covenant

_____

_____

_____

6. Exchanging names

_____

_____

_____

10. Circumcision was the external _____ of the spiritual and internal work. Circumcision, the shedding of blood, was the sign of a _____ between a man and his God.

11. The shed _____ of Jesus Christ became the sign of this new and last _____ between God and all of _____.

12. Marriage is a _____ relationship.

13. _____ is God-given and a wondrous thing. It's not something to be shunned or considered shameful. Your virginity is something you have to give to _____ person, _____ time in your life.

14. It is possible to prove the virginity of a _____, but not the virginity of a _____.

15. What makes sex sacred?

_____

_____

Chapter Four
The Wonder of Sex

Chapter Five
For the Clueless Bride

Let's Talk About Sex

1. Decide, _____ you marry, what kind of birth control, if any, you will be using.

2. What are some things you may want to have on hand before having sex?

_____

_____

_____

3. Sex (like everything else) has to be _____.

4. Our culture tends to teach women that sexual enjoyment is for _____, that "nice girls don't" or that sex is somehow _____.

5. The Word makes it clear that God designed both _____ and _____ to enjoy sex, and that liking sex is _____ and healthy.

6. Your spouse's _____ and sexuality will be _____ than yours.

7. There is usually some trepidation about the possibility of _____ at first intercourse. This is _____, but you should try to put it in perspective.

8. Most women feel _____ pain or discomfort (certainly no worse than a brief menstrual cramp), a few experience _____ pain, and a few experience _____ pain.

9. What are some things that can be done to minimize discomfort during sex?

_____

_____

_____

Chapter Five
For the Clueless Bride

10. Because of the _____ of first intercourse, and because most women do not have a good _____ of their own bodies, it is fairly normal for women not to _____ at first intercourse.

11. What are some things that you can do for your spouse during sex?

_____

_____

_____

12. What general advice is given for a sexual relationship with your spouse?

_____

_____

_____

Chapter Six
For the Clueless Groom

Let's Talk About Sex

1. Name some of the issues mentioned in this chapter that may affect sex with your wife?

_____

_____

_____

2. Men's bodies seem to _____ what to do even when our minds don't, but women don't find the same to be true. So the woman has to learn not only _____, but she also has to learn _____, _____, and _____.

3. The most important thing for you to do is to make it clear to her that you know God intends sex to be _____, _____, and _____ _____ for both of you.

4. What is one possible issue with using hormonal birth control?

_____

_____

_____

5. Too much lubricant is better than too little.

    True   False

6. Sex is like anything else, it takes _____ to get good at it, and lots of _____ to get _____ at it. The _____ you do it, the _____ it will get for both of you, in many ways.

7. For women physical _____ pleasure is a _____ response.

Chapter Six
For the Clueless Groom

8. Your wife may enjoy the _____ closeness from the very first, depending on what she is expecting, but she will need _____ to develop the ability to fully enjoy _____ physically.

9. Mixed _____ or _____ of pain the first time may make orgasm impossible, and _____ your wife to do something she can't will only make it _____.

10. What are some suggestions for lighting during sex, especially the first time?

_____

_____

_____

11. What are some things you can do to prepare your wife for sex?

_____

_____

_____

12. You should never experiment during sex with your wife.

    True   False

Chapter Seven
The Anatomy of Arousal

Let's Talk About Sex

Explain each of the stages men go through during sex.

1. Arousal

___

___

___

2. Plateau

___

___

___

3. Orgasm

___

___

___

4. Resolution

___

___

___

Chapter Seven
The Anatomy of Arousal

Explain each of the stages women go through during sex.

5. Arousal

___

___

___

6. Plateau

___

___

___

7. Orgasm

___

___

___

8. Resolution

___

___

___

Chapter Eight
Scheduling Intimacy

Let's Talk About Sex

1. The media is a good measuring stick to determine what is right or normal.

    True   False

2. Should sex always be spontaneous? Why?

_____

_____

_____

3. For the spouse with a higher desire, the fear of _____ often sets in. One becomes weary of having to _____, or even _____, for sex on a regular basis.

4. When a couple can agree upon a basic schedule for sex in marriage, it takes the _____ out.

5. What is the largest sex organ in the human body?

_____

6. Once sex is on the calendar, it provides a reminder to _____ about sex, prepares us mentally for being together physically, and primes us to "get in the _____."

7. When lovemaking is kept on the front burner, it builds _____.

8. How can sex be recreation?

_____

_____

_____

Chapter Eight
Scheduling Intimacy

7. Most couples not only differ in their desires concerning _____ of sex, but also in the _____ that's conducive to sex.

8. Preparing for sex physically helps build anticipation.

    True   False

9. If we're going to commit to lovemaking on a regular basis, we need to honor our _____ and _____. When we honor our word, it builds _____ and deepens _____.

10. In what ways can scheduling sex be beneficial?

_____

_____

_____

_____

_____

Chapter Nine
The Bridge Between Touch and Sex

Let's Talk About Sex

1. Why do babies deprived of touch not develop properly?

_____

_____

_____

2. What are some of the effects on people deprived of touch?

_____

_____

_____

3. Touch causes our bodies to produce a hormone called _____.

4. What effects does this hormone produce?

_____

_____

_____

5. Having sex—even when you don't have a drive to do so—will actually affect you in ways that will result in a _____ sex drive.

6. How can the effect of touch differ in women at different times?

_____

_____

_____

Chapter Nine
The Bridge Between Touch and Sex

7. What are some things you can do to touch more?

_____

_____

_____

Chapter Ten
Setting the Scene

List some things you can do to help set the scene in each area.

1. Privacy

___

___

___

2. Comfort

___

___

___

3. Sight

___

___

___

4. Smell

___

___

___

Chapter Ten
Setting the Scene

5. Touch

_____

_____

_____

6. Taste

_____

_____

_____

7. Afterglow

_____

_____

_____

Chapter Eleven
Sexual Stewardship

Let's Talk About Sex

1 Corinthians 7

*Now concerning the things of which you wrote to me:
It is good for a man not to touch a woman...*

1. Sex is not important to marriage.

    True   False

2. Paul is talking about being celibate _____ of marriage.

    2 Nevertheless, because of sexual immorality, let each man have his own wife, and let each woman have her own husband.

3. Paul tells us that celibacy is a gift that allows a person to better _____ the Lord—he also tells us it's the _____, not the _____.

    3 Let the husband render to his wife the affection due her, and likewise also the wife to her husband.

4. Paul is saying that we are each owed _____ by our spouse (literally a debt that is owed). It's not a favor or an option; it's _____ by the marriage covenant.

    4 The wife does not have authority over her own body, but the husband does. And likewise the husband does not have authority over his own body, but the wife does.

5. There is no gender _____ when it comes to sex in marriage.

6. A man who does not meet his wife's need for _____ intimacy cannot fulfill his obligation to her _____. This very clearly makes such an omission a _____, not a "personality difference".

    5 Do not deprive one another except with consent for a time that you may give yourselves to fasting and prayer and come together again so that Satan does not tempt you because of your lack of self-control.

7. This suggests that God considers abstaining from _____ as more severe, and a greater sacrifice, than abstaining from _____.

Chapter Eleven
Sexual Stewardship

8. If we are married, _____ is a top priority; we are expected to say _____ to things which will significantly interfere with our ability to _____ ourselves sexually.

9. The Greek word translated as "lack of self-control" here literally means "_____".

10. The Apostle seems to be saying that those who are designed to be married have not been given the _____ needed to go without sex and continue to avoid giving in to _____ sin.

6 But I say this as a concession, not as a commandment.

11. What is this verse referring to?

_____

_____

_____

7 For I wish that all men were even as I myself. But each one has his own gift from God, one in this manner and another in that.

12. Paul indicates here that celibacy is a _____.

Chapter Twelve
Is There Sex After Kids?

Let's Talk About Sex

1. You need to give yourself _____ to prioritize your marriage—and that includes finding the time and energy to _____ each other.

2. Your _____ will wait while you build your _____, but your _____ won't wait for your _____ to grow up.

3. What is a sleep date?

_____

_____

_____

4. It's necessary to discuss each spouse's _____, because they're almost certain to be _____.

5. What are some questions you can ask to learn your spouse's expectations?

_____

_____

_____

6. What can you do to romance you spouse each day?

_____

_____

_____

7. You should schedule time for sex.

    True   False

Chapter Twelve
Is There Sex After Kids?

8. What are some other ways to romance your spouse recommended by parents?

_____

_____

_____

Chapter Thirteen
What's the Big Deal with Pornography?

Let's Talk About Sex

1. What is the real intent of pornography and how does it achieve its intent?

_____

_____

_____

2. What is the origin of the word "pornography"?

_____

_____

_____

3. In the United States, what criteria is used to determine whether material is obscene?

_____

_____

_____

4. The first phase of a man being ensnared by pornography is what we call "The _____" or _____ phase.

5. When a man's sight engages his sex drive, a chemical is released in his brain called _____.

6. At the point of seeing a visual stimulus, nothing immoral has occurred.

    True   False

7. As men we have a choice: _____ these images or catalogue them in our mental _____.

54

Chapter Thirteen
What's the Big Deal with Pornography?

8. What is the second phase of pornography?

_____

9. When a man has given place in his heart and soul to the pictures, images, or fantasies he has filed away in his mental library; when he recalls those images and uses them for sexual pleasure; when a man makes for himself an _____.

   Deuteronomy 4:15-16

   You saw no form of any kind the day the Lord spoke to you at Horeb out of the fire. Therefore watch yourselves very carefully, so that you do not become corrupt and make for yourselves an idol, an image of any shape, whether formed like a man or a woman.

10. The third phase of the bondage of pornography is found in the _____ it has in your life.

11. A man's mind is a place where he is supposed to go to worship _____.

12. Habitual masturbation that culminates in the sacrifice of your manhood, or seed, to the idol or pictures in a man's mind is private _____ _____.

13. What are some ways you can tell pornography has become an idol in a man's life?

_____

_____

_____

14. The final phase of a man's descent into a hell of his own making is the _____ Phase, a personal _____ of his own making.

15. Sin promises to _____ and _____, but in reality it _____ and _____.

James 1:14-15

But each one is tempted when, by his own (lust) evil desire, he is dragged away and enticed. Then, after desire has conceived, it gives birth to sin; and sin, when it is full-grown, gives birth to death.

16. Pornography will destroy your _____, your _____, and your ability to communicate and have _____ intimate relationships.

17. The greatest intimacy a man and woman will ever know in their relationship will come out of times of _____ together.

18. List the twelve steps to freedom from pornography.

_____

_____

_____

_____

_____

_____

_____

_____

_____

_____

Chapter Thirteen
What's the Big Deal with Pornography?

19. The greatest thing you will have to do to overcome the sin of pornography is to _____ spiritually.

20. What are ten things you can incorporate into your spiritual life?

_____

_____

_____

_____

_____

_____

_____

_____

_____

_____

Chapter Fourteen
Toxic Sex

Let's Talk About Sex

1. Pornography takes sex outside of the context of the protective commitment of a marriage relationship.

    True   Fales

2. There were _____ porn video titles last year versus _____ movie releases from Hollywood last year.

3. The porn culture tells you that _____, _____, and _____ are all the same thing.

4. What are some of the lies portrayed by the porn industry?

_____

_____

_____

_____

5. Everyone who sees porn will become addicted.

    True   False

6. What are the stages a porn addict goes through?

_____

_____

_____

Chapter Fourteen
Toxic Sex

_____

7. When overcoming a pornography addiction, the first thing you've got to do is _____ that you struggle with pornography.

8. There is only so much you can do in fighting addiction without help.

    True   False

9. Sin not only _____ us, but it _____ us from God.

10. In your search for _____ and _____, pornography is an empty _____ for real love.

Chapter Fifteen
Infidelity - It's More Than Just Sex

Let's Talk About Sex

1. Adultery does not have to be sexual.

    True   Fales

2. Infidelity, unfaithfulness, and adultery is any _____ or _____ intimacy that violates _____.

3. What are the three elements of inappropriate relationships?

_____

_____

_____

4. What steps can you take to affair-proof your marriage?

_____

_____

_____

_____

_____

_____

_____

Chapter Fifteen
Infidelity - It's More Than Just Sex

Chapter Sixteen
Once Gay Always Gay?

Let's Talk About Sex

1. What is typically said about people who leave a heterosexual lifestyle for a homosexual lifestyle

_____

_____

_____

2. In contrast, what is typically said about people who leave the homosexual lifestyle for the heterosexual lifestyle?

_____

_____

_____

3. Is the gay gene theory true? Who proved or disproved it?

_____

4. As children, from where do we receive our affirmation, identity, and self-worth?

_____

5. What can happen if we do not receive that affirmation from our fathers?

_____

_____

_____

6. So instead of desiring to please our father in a healthy relationship, we can create an _____ relationship through the _____ of another male through a _____ act.

Chapter Sixteen
Once Gay Always Gay?

7. This behavior becomes a learned _____, and the more it is _____, the more _____ and _____ it is perceived to be.

8. Being gay has two sides to it: the _____ (the inner needs to be met) and the _____ (using _____ to meet those needs).

9. A homosexual man can change when the original _____ needs that drove him into the lifestyle are met in a _____ way.

10. What are some of the steps that can be taken to exit a homosexual lifestyle?

_____

_____

_____

_____

_____

11. The level of _____ will depend on the level of _____ to persevere and to ride out the obstacles that one may have to face.

Chapter Seventeen
Gays in School: The Homosexual Agenda in Education

Let's Talk About Sex

1. One of the major goals of GLSEN (Gay, Lesbian and Straight Educational Network) is to _____ curricula and teaching, so that _____ themes are always _____ and always presented in a _____ manner.

2. What are some of the workshops held by GLSEN?

_____

_____

_____

3. In 2002, GLSEN held a seminar to teach _____ teachers how to explore gender, even "_____ gender," by _____.

4. What are some of the preschool level reading books supplied by GLSEN?

_____

_____

_____

5. Some curricula put _____ in a role-playing exercise where they become _____ and must _____ to things said about them.

6. Who sometimes funds GLSEN sponsored seminars for educators and students?

_____

Chapter Seventeen
Gays in School: The Homosexual Agenda in Education

7. What can you do to fight the introduction of a homosexual agenda in your child's education?

_____

_____

_____

Chapter Eighteen
The Homosexual Agenda

Let's Talk About Sex

1. In his article in *The Advocate*, Steve Warren made his demands negotiable.

    True   False

2. What are some of the demands made by Warren in this article?

_____

_____

_____

_____

3. What is Warren's final warning?

_____

_____

_____

Chapter Eighteen
The Homosexual Agenda

Let's Talk About Sex

Chapter Nineteen
The Homosexual Manifesto

Let's Talk About Sex

1. Swift's Manifesto is hostile towards those who hold a Biblical view against homosexuality.

   True   False

2. What are some of the things that have happened since the writing of the homosexual manifesto?

   _____

   _____

   _____

   _____

   _____

3. How does this reveal that some of Swift's ideas may be gaining ground?

   _____

   _____

   _____

Chapter Nineteen
The Homosexual Manifesto

Let's Talk About Sex

Chapter Twenty
Fatherhood Aborted

Let's Talk About Sex

1. What three things is a man created by God to do for his family?

_____

_____

_____

_____

_____

2. When a man is a willing or unwilling participant in the taking of a life that he was created and called to father, love, and raise, it _____ his soul in ways that are _____ and—outside of Christ—_____ to deal with.

3. The promoters of the abortion industry have everyone convinced that abortion is _____, simple, easy, and no one gets _____.

4. When, according to the Supreme Court, does a father receive parental rights?

_____

_____

_____

5. What symptoms may a post-abortive man have?

_____

_____

_____

Chapter Twenty
Fatherhood Aborted

6. What other behaviors may be seen in post-abortive men?

_____

_____

_____

Let's Talk About Sex

Chapter Twenty-One
When Daddy's Dream Died, Daddy Died Too

Let's Talk About Sex

1. What percentage of women are having more than one abortion?

   _____

2. The most comprehensive study to date involved a thousand men who completed questionnaires in thirty different abortion clinics as they waited for their partner's abortion, after which follow-up occurred. The result showed that _____ percent or more have been deeply traumatized by the abortion.

3. God has blessed man with a desire to _____ for and _____ his family.

4. When an abortion takes place, these crucial, God-given instincts are often _____ or totally obliterated.

5. In addition to anger, a man might experience _____, _____, _____, and _____.

6. Many post-abortive men are apprehensive about being involved in another pregnancy.

   True   False

7. What are some other effects men may experience after being involved in an abortion?

   _____

   _____

   _____

8. A crucial aspect of post-abortion counseling is the realization of divine _____.

**Chapter Twenty-One
When Daddy's Dream Died, Daddy Died Too**

Help for Dads

What if it's too late to prevent an abortion? What if my partner had one without my knowledge or consent? How do I deal with the stress and depression associated with abortion?

Here are some organizations that provide counseling services or other resources for dealing with abortion issues.

Care Net
109 Carpenter Drive, Suite 100
Sterling, VA 20164
(703) 478-5661x33
www.care-net.org

Healing a Father's Heart: A Post-Abortion Bible Study for Men by Cochren and Jones

Fathers & Brothers Ministries
350 Broadway, Suite 40
Boulder, CO 80303
(303) 494-3282

Fatherhood Forever Foundation
3851 E. Thunderbird Road #111-254
Phoenix, AZ 85032-5720
(602) 334-7651
fatherhoodforever.org

Fatherhood Forever has a growing list of those who counsel fathers of aborted babies

Life Issues Institute

1821 W Galbraith Road
Cincinnati, OH 45239
(513) 729-3600
www.lifeissues.org

Referral network for men via web site and phone.
"Missing Arrows" A Bible Study for Men by Warren Williams
Brochure, "Men Hurt Too"
Presentation, "Can You Hear Their Pain?"

Wayne F. Brauning

Men's Abortion Recovery Ministries
5021 Newhall Street
Philadelphia, PA 19144

Brochure, "Men & The Big Picture"

House of Esau Ministries

12 Craglea Corner
Winnipeg, Manitoba, Canada
R2C 4L2
www.silverlion.org/publications.html

Brochures, PowerPoint Presentation

Websites of Interest:

www.pureintimacy.org
www.xxxchurch.com
www.netaccountability.com
www.covenanteyes.com

Resources of Interest

Character is King
Dr. John Binkley

It's a Guy Thing: Character is King takes you on your dream journey. There is a place called destiny that we all journey to. We all have ideas, dreams and vision for what life should be. This book lays out a plan for that journey to realizing your dreams, and to your destiny.

Let's Talk About Sex
Dr. John A. King

Let's face it. Sexuality is all around us. It's even on billboards, magazines and television commercials. Sadly, It's a topic many men and women have to deal with on their own because too many churches or pastors won't touch it. Find out what the Bible has to say about some of the toughest questions in *Let's Talk About Sex*.

Now to Next
Dr. John A. King

What does the next generation church look like? Who are the people that will be involved in the next generation church? How will it come about?

Those are some of the questions answered in Dr. King's newest release, *Now to Next: Blueprint for a Christian Revolution.*

Helping Guys Become Men, Husbands, and Fathers
Dr. John A. King

It's a Guy Thing takes you on the journey of fatherhood. Dr. John King shares the skills necessary to become a good father. He shows you what can happen when a father is absent or simply not active in a child's life. Being a male is a matter of birth. Being a man is a matter of choice. This book will help you make that choice.

To see all the titles available through Guy Thing Press, visit us online at www.guythingpress.com

Resources of Interest

Business By The Book
Dr. John A. King

The world's greatest handbook on leadership, economic and social excellence is not found in schoolbooks, but in Scripture. The principles in this book are tried, proven and resilient over centuries. Christ bet His life on it, and so can you.

Show Me the Money
Dr. John A. King

Time Magazine asked, "Does God want you to be rich?" The answer to that question is simply "No, God wants you to be *wealthy*." In *Show Me the Money*, you will learn the fundamentals of creating and using wealth in God's kingdom.

Achieving Authentic Wealth
Jeff McLoud

We need a vision that goes beyond our ability to be consumers only. A vision so big, so powerful, that we cannot even accomplish it in our own lifetime - a vision founded from the very heartbeat of God. We could see the vision fulfilled if we ask ourselves a simple question: "How can we achieve twice as much with half the money?"

Creating a Better Life
Erik A. Kudlis

In this easy to read manual, educator and administrator turned international businessman, Erik Kudlis, identifies three vital keys you must know and use, given by God Himself, that unlock the doors to the life God has always wanted you to have.

To see all the titles available through Guy Thing Press, visit us online at www.guythingpress.com

Further Resources

The Godly Man Curriculum

The Godly Man Curriculum is designed to train men from all walks of life, giving them a firm foundation of doctrine and Godly knowledge. This curriculum is available both over the internet for individual study and on DVD for seminars, Sunday schools, and men's meetings. With up to 7 hours of video teaching divided over numerous topics, the Godly Man Curriculum is an excellent tool that you can build your classes upon and grow yourself and your people.

Listen to sample teachings from the Godly Man Curriculum at www.imnonline.org.

Building Iron Men & Life As Leaders Networks

The Building Iron Men and Life as Leaders networks are two of IMN's finest resources. Each network provides you with a new teaching every month that will challenge and encourage you to grow. The Building Iron Men network features three teachings in both CD and DVD format that are tailored for men, while the Life as Leaders network provides you with three CDs that teach leadership principles anyone can use.

Both networks are phenomenal tools that are vital assets to any church and discipleship program.

Also check out these websites for great resources and training materials.

International Men's Network
www.imnonline.org

Guy Thing Press
www.guythingpress.com

The International Men's Network was founded by Dr. John A. King. Its purpose is to help men grow to become the leaders their families and churches need and become men of God that make a lasting impact on those around them.

IMN is a missionary organization to the men of the world. We are committed to:

- Inspire all men to rise to a high standard of biblical manhood.
- Encourage them to excel in their roles as men, leaders, husbands, and fathers.
- Challenge them to be contributors to society and set an example based upon a biblical value system that will benefit this generation and lay a solid foundation for the next generation.

The International Men's Network is dedicated to providing and hosting the best resources for men, including teachings and lessons on CD and DVD and conferences that teach men the principles that will help them become more influential and effective in their lives.

For more information about IMN and its mission, visit us online at www.imnonline.org or call 817.993.0047

The Christian Life Center was founded by Dr. John King and his wife, Beccy. With a vision to preach the gospel of Jesus Christ with unashamed passion and uncompromising truth, Christian Life Center aims to raise up the next generation of leaders to move into all the world and proclaim the truth of Christ to the lost and broken.

Located in the Keller, Texas area, the church sits in the prime location to reach the community and the people therein. The church desires to give back to the community by providing outreaches to better and enrich its inhabitants. From kickboxing classes that are aimed at teaching children and adults self-defense, to a special service that commemorates and honors our country's war-time heroes, Christian Life Center strives to bring a living Jesus to a dying world by new and imaginative means that will bless and change lives.

For more information about Christian Life Center and the resources it offers, visit the website at www.clctx.org